COV KIDS
ANTONY OWEN

Newton-le-Willows

Published in the United Kingdom in 2021
by The Knives Forks And Spoons Press,
51 Pipit Avenue,
Newton-le-Willows,
Merseyside,
WA12 9RG.

ISBN 978-1-912211-79-1

Copyright © Antony Owen 2021.

The right of Antony Owen to be identified as the author of this work has been asserted by them in accordance with the Copyrights, Designs and Patents Act of 1988. All rights reserved. No part of this publication may be reproduced, stored in a retrieval system, transmitted in any form or by any means, electronic, photocopying, recording or otherwise, without prior permission of the publisher.

Acknowledgements:

Some of these poems have appeared in: *WORD, The Brown Envelope Book* by Culture Matters, *The Bread & Roses Anthology of Working-Class Poetry* (Culture Matters), *10:10 Press: The Working Class Anthology*, *Bogside* (An Anthology of Peace Poets), *The Echo Room, Bogman's Cannon, Atrium, Grey Town, Live Encounters, I Am Not a Silent Poet*.

The poem 'If Boris Johnson Had a Cuppa with my Nan from Willenhall' was a 2020 Bread & Roses Poetry Award Winner (sponsored by Unite).

Thanks to: National Poetry Day & BBC for commissioning "I Jaguar" (2016); the BBC CWR for featuring the Cyrille Regis tribute poem on their community show and Coventry City Football Club for featuring it on their website and in their match day programme; Leicester NHS Partnership, Word & Film maker Leonie DuBarry-Gurr for the Cyrille Regis Video; and the Positive Images Festival 2020 for funding workshops based on some of these poems.

For Leanne Bridgewater
our Cov Kid

*"So, you lost today team, but look at the positives:
you saw the match through and are covered head to toe in mud,
so why can't I see you covered in pride for trying your best?"*

– Random bloke called Coach at Coundon Park, Coventry, shouting
to his Under 11 side after they lost 6-1 to a team from Solihull.

Contents

Foreword	9
Love Poem: Letter for Ordinary People	13
Phillip Larkin's Mistress	14
Park Lane Nightclub	15
Mr Porky's	16
The House Three Doors from My Nan's	17
Sunset Over a Stabbed Boy	18
If Boris Johnson Had a Cuppa with My Nan from Willenhall	19
Keresley Girl	20
On the Pull in the Nineties	21
Calling Out Racism Coventry Style	22
Cyrille Regis	23
Ska Blue	24
Two Men Talk Politics Bollocks at Coffee Architects	25
The Night David Bowie Died	26
I Was Born as Bowie Sang From Mars	27
My Nan Was a Cov Kid Who Died Dreaming	28
Love in the Age of Lockdown	29
Dear IKEA from the Cov Kids	30
I, Jaguar	31
Cov Kids	32
Memoirs of Job Seeker NZ328509B	33
Paradise in Amazon	34
The Brave Leave Willingly	35
A Teacher's Suicide	36
Before the Rain Came	37
Closing Libraries in The City of Culture	38
Coventry Street	40
Daily Mail	41
The Most Beautiful Cov Kids	42
Coventry Zoo	43
Some Famous Cov Kids	44
Poems for People Who Never Read Them	45
Rebellion Song	46

Foreword
by Joseph Horgan

One of my Irish immigrant father's enduring habits was the buying of an Irish newspaper whilst living in England. News from home rooted him, momentarily, in a foreign place. This Irishman adrift in England. This uprooted man. This immigrant. *Cov Kids*, by comparison, seems to be a complete contrast to that. A Coventry man writing poems about Coventry. A Cov Kid writing about Cov Kids. Writing a celebration of place. A particular place, a particular culture, a particular way of life. Writing the local. But in that very moment, in that very essence of local, it is more. Far, far more. It is the local in order to see the local, yes, but also the national, the international, the others. The human. Another Irishman, the poet Patrick Kavanagh, would have recognized all of this. 'All great civilizations are based on parochialism,' Kavanagh succinctly wrote. Everything is local and in the local is everything. My immigrant father is reading his Irish newspaper and sitting next to him someone is reading *Cov Kids*.

These pages, these local lines, are not patterned with the tiny, fluttering, dispirited flags of patriotism; that retreat of the incessantly insecure. The gaze of *Cov Kids* is beyond all of that. In celebrating his home, in focusing on such intimate details, Owen's purpose is not the narrowing of the camera's angle. Each minute moment, each calibrated line, each lovingly written take on the street, only ever leads to the camera panning out. It only ever brings us to the camera incorporating all these streets, all the ring roads, all the concrete blocks, all the cities, and, most of all, most, most of all, all the people. In reporting back from the instant, the immediate, the focus of *Cov Kids* becomes that of the enduring. Another Irish poet Michael Longley said, 'if I knew where poems came from, I'd go there.' *Cov Kids* makes its own assertion in that regard. It takes the humble front room, the despairing nightclub, a biscuit tin, racism, football, pop music, lost boys and girls, IKEA, and all the unmentionable signifiers of class. And it says this is where poems come from.

Patrick Kavanagh also wrote of poetry that 'material itself has no special value.' The majestic valley is no more poetic than the rundown pastry shop. The spilling out from a 2am nightclub is no less poetic than the arboretum on the country estate. What matters with the material, Kavanagh says, 'is what our imagination and our love do to it.' Poems aren't waiting in some special, anointed place, some valley only poets know the coordinates for. Where the poems are depends on where you're looking. And, of course, on who's doing the looking.

Antony Owen

If poetry doesn't like most people, and it doesn't, does it, too refined, too particular, too aware of itself, too clean and too clever, to be spending time with the bingo players, and the dangerous dog walkers, and the tracksuit wearers, and the petrol station attendants, and the fast food outlet servers, and the readers of the back pages of the newspaper, and the grim, unimaginative lives of the wage dependent, then poetry's a parlor game played by the self-anointed for the self-serving. If, though, poetry is laced with the imagination and love Kavanagh pinpointed, it becomes the so-called crazy man on the street corner, nodding his head as everyone passes by, seeing it all, recognizing it all, knowing it all, writing it all. Writing it all down.

Men like my father, immigrants, dependent on overtime, wage worried, laughing, night shift workers, don't wander these shelves of poetry. They don't need to see it written down that Only Poets with Clean Hands Win Prizes. They live that every day. If they did though, if the bus home was late and to get out of the rain they went in the nearest door, and there by chance found themselves in the poetry aisles, they might peruse a spine or two, lift a copy here and another further on, and putting them back turn to go and hesitate, turn back and pick up, just by chance you understand, Cov Kids, they'd flick it open, look at the words, the line, grasp the rhythm, and say, ah yeh, here, look, now, yes, I didn't imagine I would, but I recognise this.

COV KIDS

Rangzeb Hussain

Cov Kids

Love ~~Poem~~: Letter for Ordinary People
For Terry & Roxanne

When I'm comfy on the sofa I would get up and walk to the Co-op and buy you a Twix™ and a mini Prosecco.™ I would watch *Come Dancing*™ with you and pluck dried baby sick from your hair like gold sieved from a settler's hands. When the cat sidles into our thighs I would stroke him wrong so he chooses you and you'd say: "HA! He chose me over you." I'd do that for you, because you'd fuckin' love it.™

I would say "fuckin' love it" in a poem so no one would publish it, because it's for you and only you. So it only needs to be engraved like a cheap Pandora™ charm around your boxing glove heart that punches your chest for me and only me. I fuckin' love it when I know I'm getting older, but you say I'm silver haired because – like the moon scuffed in the ripped skyline – there is a beauty that keeps getting better.

When we're so fuckin old and comfy on the sofa I'll rub E45™ into your scalp and tell you that if I could walk to the Co-op I'd buy you a bottle of whiskey to take us back to the night we laughed our heads off at the sadness of our lives. I remember that night we heard an echo in the house and years later a baby filled it like the nest in the bony bough of my tired chest where a heart beats like yolk for you.

I'm gonna die with you a hundred times and feel the tickly flower stems our children leave at our grave knowing we made them happy. I'm gonna live with you once (yeah, just the once) and then we'll be atoms smashing into sky.

13

Antony Owen

Phillip Larkin's Mistress

If I met Cov in the thumbnails of Tinder
she'd ride naked from an ungroomed nag and smoke like Bette Davis.
Peeping Tom's would be blinded by her beauty and 'don't give a flying-fuck' vibe.

If I met Earl Leofric in Park Lane Nightclub I would challenge him to a duel.
We'd both take ten paces, then I'd shoot back tequila and salt.
I'd defend Godiva from the ass that wants to ride her.

God help me, but if I met Phillip Larkin fixing his bike chain at his mistresses
I would ask him if his true love is Hull and tell him of our oils:
Black / white two-tones mixing to grey, washing him clean.

Park Lane Nightclub
For Pete Barr

We used to sneak *Mad Dog* past bouncers with blue and pink fists that shone like shit discos at Bobbie's Club when Spandau filled dance floors covered in glass, and teeth of a danced over pretty boy. We used to get our hands stamped in Park Lane and after a slash in kebab filled urinals we'd wash our hands but keep that badge dry so we could stay inside till the ink went. Each week, when a fight broke out, I'd cop off with the same different girl and I'd try to kiss her properly in burgundy stay-press, saying something like Swayze would whisper to Baby in the lake scene. We used to fear the last dance and being left with the men in Gino Manchini sweaters. And it was anyone for anyone. Then on to Mr Porky's, or chips and a row at the Parsons. We used to drink Babycham in Memory Lane, where posh girls licked salt from our piss stained hands and downed the best tequila with a tinned olive. I remember one night a woman punched a man out cold for dry humping her as Billy Ocean crooned, and when he came around she made sure he heard that he was a knobhead and had no class coz he was, in her words, a fucking dirty arsehole. We used to save all week to cram into a yellowed TR7 with go fast stripes and act really cool as it coughed its way into the city. We used to snog girls and wonder through the epic process if they'd go halves on a taxi back to our place, and if Mum would be up watching re-runs of *Dynasty* on the Amstrad portable. We used to worry about that a lot, then realise the girl we were kissing was not really interested and thinking the same thing without letting us in to her place coz our hands rolled around her like piss-game fag butts in urinals. We used to think how cool it was to blow smoke into a girl's face and think she must have liked it coz we're dressed like Don Johnson from the bloke at Ciro Citterio who resembled Terry from Brookside saying we looked really fuckin cool in Miami Vice peach and vanilla. I used to think in Park Lane nightclub that one day I'd write a poem about this place and this is not its coz there weren't a poem to be written. I often think that Park Lane nightclub was the place to be, but now it's a TJ Hughes, so in its Caff I'll ask for a tequila in the very spot they used to serve it and she'll look at me not having a clue what I'm on about and then, just for a second, Park Lane never closed.

Antony Owen

Mr Porky's

Come shave me a Cov ribbon at Mr Porky's.
We are known for our ribbons, oh weaver of crackling.
I was the king of Pink Parrots dance floor tonight so let me feast.
Spoon me apple slop with a gloveless hand, pass me greasy change and E. coli.

We don't care about five-star hygiene, just pork bobbing in tinfoil china.
Ignore the slurred fight politics of soccer and who Ray copped off with,
she just wants a pork and stuffing batch and to watch VHS in streetlight.
It's time to whistle a cab and burn pink marks on our legs as we dine Cov style.

The House Three Doors from My Nan's

"Cov kids have a fire in them and that comes from the blitz"
  — Coventry Evacuee

In the loft three doors from my Nan's a bomb fell over Joyce.
The father crawled out holding his severed hand.
A woman told him to cover his privates.
He was talking shock gibberish.

In the exposed pantry the torn lungs of gas pipes gargled.
Someone commented on how nice the wallpaper was.
A dog snapped at the burst water mains barking,
then the question was asked: "Where's Joyce?"

The nosey parker didn't want to look and got her Ted.
He found a purple bag of bones swaying on a beam.
"I've found her," he yelled, "Poor old cow."
"Don't fuckin come in here," he pleaded.

My Nan was unscathed, just pinioned like a shrew in a cat's paw.
She was a driver of three carriages that wailed without stopping.
Maggie, Victor, Patricia, all of my kin staring into exposed houses,
asking: "Why does it smell of eggs and fish on the turn?"

Antony Owen

Sunset Over a Stabbed Boy
For Fidel & Neville

For you,
dusk lifts the dead weight of day.
Horizon spills her stars into the pail of your mouth.
You can sleep now, it is all over and a gentle silence comes.

For you,
the Ska union of crow and dove,
a sparrow-hawk in its blood-mist does not comfort.
There are some birds that destroy nests and all they ever gave.

For you,
a new song from an old black throat.
These are the hymns of your unlived life.
Your uncle knows of scar and Ska and birds in migration.

Migrate in the blood-warm rivulets you leave on Coventry stone.
You are not about the violence and all about light after dark.

If Boris Johnson Had a Cuppa with My Nan from Willenhall

I picture Boris arriving at my Nan's with a spray of daffs from Esso.
She'd nail off the price and thank him with the oil of her lips.
This is not a fair trade, for my Nan was a street fighter.

She'd offer him a seat, the only one, and she would sit on the ottoman.
He would crack a joke about Turks and she would laugh at him.
She'd laugh at him every time he spoke and when he did not.

My Nan would offer him broken biscuits from the market and he'd decline.
She would break open the family circle box and offer him the best,
he would decline and war would be declared now that they're open.

"You come in my fuckin house with limp dick daffs, sit on my dead man's chair,
quip racist jokes, turn your nose up at my broken biscuits, you flopsy fucker.
You let me open the good stuff and let the air get to them, you ungrateful sod."

"Those daffs are your policies; those broken biscuits are Brexit; that ottoman is Britain,
stuffed with different colours, with whites on the top; and that tea was from Amritsar,
and it will stain your teeth like bullets fop-haired men like you gave orders to fire."

If Boris Johnson had tea with my Nan there would be anarchy in a teacup.

Antony Owen

Keresley Girl
For Jo

Once upon a time in the ghost-town grey we kissed and
it was softer than the boxers fist I taped before he was knocked out.
Yeah, you knocked me out in round one and here we still are fighting life.

Something about Keresley girls that makes the Cov boys melt –
remember how snowflakes felt on your lips the first time?
It's okay to melt from a kiss made with such love.

The thing with Cov girls is that they come from a blitz,
we are made to melt upon their pale hearths of skin:
it is a safe place, a dangerous place, *but your place*.

The thing with Cov girls is that they'll share a kebab with ya,
they will share an Uber with ya and maybe their bed.
But, if you cross em they will end you with a glance.

On the Pull in the Nineties

In the nineties we stopped tucking our shirts in,
lads wove like crap disco lights in Ben Sherman,
Cov was a grey Serengeti of frizzy hair and straight-talking.

I remember there was a secret way of impressing a Cov girl:
you told em that were not from Cov and acted mysterious,
the truth is that you were from Cov in every fuckin way.

We used to have The Irish Centre filled to the brim like a badly pulled Guinness.
If you hadn't copped off by the last dance you were nothing.
I remember that's when insults were thrown. *Then bottles*.

We used to feel all posh queuing up at the Skydome when it opened.
The Council hung a banner from the crane embarrassing us forever:
"SKYDOME OPENING SOON – SORRY BIRMINGHAM."

I remember in Jumpin' Jaks all the theorists at the confessional urinals:
"I fuckin' love her mate sheeeezzz blowing me out innit fuckin bitch."
I remember trying to piss quicker and trying to escape the cologne peddler.

As for that cologne peddler in Chicago Rocks who called it "Pussy juice,"
I remember an old swinger saying he "should show more fuckin' respect."
He then punched him out and was dragged out by men you never, ever, eyed.

Antony Owen

Calling Out Racism Coventry Style

To remove spit off a windscreen you need white vinegar:
it neutralises their stench when the heater kicks in.
Then we wake the kids, so they're none the wiser –
until ghosts of condensation scrawl go home n ...

To remove excrement from a letterbox you need a screwdriver.
Detach the black bristle draught excluder and lob it in the bin.
Scrub the mechanism in a bucket of bleach,
wear rubber gloves, your eyes may water.

To remove a human being from the area: repeat hate over,
teach racism to your child (for this is learnt behaviour),
send Christmas cards of two refugees on a donkey
to xenophobes who cry at John Lewis ads.

To remove a racist from the whole country, call them out.
Next week this two-tone street snow will melt,
like blood. It shall flow to the gutter as music.
Everyone and no one will care, repeat over.

Cyrille Regis

French Guiana-born, you learnt how to charge through bananas like mist.
Those slave-lands were your anchor to run and live free.
I picture a leather ball as your chair beneath sunsets.

In West Bromwich you learnt from shoelaces the smell of England,
the puree of banana, saliva and the soiled chalk of white men.
You shrugged them off like an own goal to decency.

You were the uncaged magpie, a song against the bulldog's snarl,
more than a black man, but a human who silenced the noise,
the smiling tower on bedroom walls of proud black boys.

In Coventry came a magpie, a sky-blue heart in a city Thatcher greyed.
You charged through the right wing to Kop-song murmuration's.
Each time you played, win or lose, was an unknown celebration.

In Liverpool you became a liver-bird with a frond of the Magpies blue.
Monsters made monkey noises, but you never walked alone,
they took you in like bird-song, like one of their own.

Your first England cap when they posted you cowardice in a bullet and ink,
"If you put your foot on Wembley turf, you'll get one for your knees."
How sweet the grass of England and the black defiant rose.

Guiana-born, you learnt your first steps charging through the foggy flora.
The best pass your Father made was from your Mother at birth.
He must have felt he'd won, that ball of life now returned to earth.

Antony Owen

Ska Blue
For Pru

Here is where weavers whisper all things Coventry:
the patois of sky-blue rain in two-tone sky;
running from the Sherbourne, free
from torrent to restful sigh.

Here is where Godiva rode to move equality forward:
from *Cofa's Tree* across the ley to *Coventre*.
Her body fragrant as the old Abbot orchard,
wild as the taupe ribbon Sowe and free.

Here is where our blitz turned eyes to red stained glass,
where sky moaned for all that would pass,
and children boarded trains to strangers
to sleep in cold and unfamiliar mangers.

Here is where our new skin became two-tone grey:
mix black and white, for this is who we are.
Not brutalist skin, but tender within.
Pure as music in rain and Ska.

Here is where you shall leave your mark today.
Child of two-tone music, there's good in grey.
There is good in the rivers of our blood.
We are Cov and this is our day.

Two Men Talk ~~Politics~~ Bollocks at Coffee Architects

In Royal Leamington Spa
it is raining Siamese cats and French Poodles.
Ten miles away in Coventry it is pissing it down and
someone calls my city violent, yet rain makes crowns in puddles there.

In Royal Leamington Spa
people queue in the rain to feel middle class.
The hazing begins and I get a seat by the window.
I see a beggar hold out her cap to feel the payment of soft April rain.

Two men discuss the election, sprinkling Palestinian herbs like mortars,
occupied like the window seat the foppish man stole.
Nobody saw him steal it because it was the norm,
and who fucking cares if it aint COVID or *TOWIE?*

Antony Owen

The Night David Bowie Died

The first girl I French kissed tasted of Indian summer rain.
It came later than expected, but when it came I was pure.
David Bowie's voice flew across the cinema in octaves.
He brought my lips to hers like a stray dog scratching a closed door.

The second girl I kissed bit my lips to be cool and Madonna.
I pushed her over and her dress was covered in dogshit.
She later threw a drink in my face to be edgy and Mandinka.
I was lost in my headphones trying to find Major Tom.

The night David Bowie died my wife and I laid in silence.
A moth bounced against the filament like wood on drumskin
and we talked about how cancer can never really eat us.
We played *This is not America* on repeat, then kissed like husband and wife.

I Was Born as Bowie Sang From Mars
For Sarah, Toni & Max

In the babbling brook of my birth I knew that women were harbours
and I was the boat attached to a cord getting lost as they cut us apart.
In the deep blue sea of my birth-eyes I drank the sour milk of night sky
and my Father swam there as he took in the salt of his shipwrecked son.

I know this of sons and daughters: they are islands claimed by sea,
and why I am drawn to the pull of the ocean was never beyond me.
I know this of broken waters: they are violence maimed by breeze,
and why, when I was torn from the hull of her ocean, I was brought to my knees.

On the earthquake of my Grandfather's chest I heard his crow black heart
lifting mockingbirds drenched in tar from years of knockoff cigarettes.
In the deep blue sea of his collar I floated like wild geese over Willenhall,
where one of my friends was made by the lake in a stolen Ford Capri.

I know this of my birth: I was born as Bowie sang all the way from Mars.
And, as I entered earth around Dawn, a snowy owl flew through burnt-out cars.
I know this of my life: I have yet to watch the geese fly over Willenhall Wood.
Gonna take my wife and fall on my knees, yeah, she'll dab away the blood.

In the cracked beds of my Father's face I know why men are shipwrecks:
they sailed by the *Blackstar* Bowie found in masts of deathbed cotton;
they floated away like Ford Granadas down newly tarmacked streets,
where lost boys like me always ended up, with David Jones and Bowie in Mars.

Antony Owen

My Nan Was a Cov Kid Who Died Dreaming

I was four when I saw my Nan lying dead in the foetal position, delivered in her sleep to the primordial skin of sky. My Mum tapped at the window, with her blue hairy breath shrivelling like a dead violet on the window. We three brothers sat in our duffel coats sobbing because our Mum was, and because we knew death was all about the colour blue. Flesh blue. Veins blue. Breaths blue. The policeman blue. Daimler blue. Sirens blue. Mother blue. Our tongues after a Slush Puppy blue. My Mother's Mother was the kind of woman who could turn a tin of spam into a meal for six and could stretch a spud from Monday to Thursday with breadcrumbs the birds never got to see. I remember my Mother's Father-in-law holding my Mum without their bodies coming into contact and when he said "God" my Mum turned the windscreen wipers on for no reason and then Tony Blackburn up full volume because my Mum loved her mum and absolutely hated Tony Blackburn, except then, then he was God.

Love in the Age of Lockdown

In Valencia
thin birds return to the barrio.
An old lady who knows this silence ties nuts from her balcony.
This is her act of love for birdsong, for the marshes they bring to her.

In Brittany
a rich man's Gite is broken into.
They will never know it was a fox.
She went there because barbarians dug up her den as her kits slept.

In London Zoo
wolves excite the silent air,
then soda lights ignite and steal the full moon from them.
It matters not, for a poet heard the cry and captured it to free them.

In Baghdad
a widow lets her husband fly.
The colour of his eyes thrown to wind.
Nothing is said.

Near Leamington
a pigeon smashed into my wing mirror.
It was just like a dirty angel had died in its own rain.
I went to pick it up, but a magpie came to drink from its heart and I let it.

In Guantanamo Bay
they cannot stop the scent of white mariposa.
It enters the cells and makes the prisoners smile:
the pharmacist, the soldier, the carpenter, the erased.

Antony Owen

Dear IKEA from the Cov Kids
After Spoz

You killed Liquid Café with your fifty pence offer.
Mario Petrucci read his poetry there and you should know.
His words were ballads of Chernobyl and places we've embraced:
Srebrenica, Lidice, Dresden, the pre-Brexit favelas, and Alms rejects.
Mario Petrucci was like City Arcade Canaries, exotic and colourful,
with his retch-yellow corpses of sweat striped miners of scythe and sickle.
Remember, IKEA, you have no soul, not like Mario Petrucci in the Liquid.

You killed Fishy Moores and their curling cod in mead-batter and lemon.
Those machine-cut meatballs defrosting in oil like fat war criminals in saunas,
that patriotic Daim Bar cheesecake that gave me a high to buy flatpack.
Go jut that flagpole into Godiva's sky-blue heart and punch her pure horse.
The sun will burn over the hole you leave like Peeping Tom's eye-socket.
Go fuck yourself and take your bullshit philanthropic robe of gold rags,
for we have rebuilt a whole city with instructions less confusing than yours.
So, go fuck yourself IKEA. And when you go, the pigeons will return us to grey.

IKEA
Go fuck yourself.

Sincerely,

Cov Kid No: 2098663201

I, Jaguar

I was made in Cov by men who drank ale and cocoa,
who lived as close as Browns Lane and dreamt a basic dream.
On Sundays they petrol-mowed their tiger-striped lawns, then
drove to church in bashed up suits and rusty, wheezing cars.

I was made in Cov by women who made cocoa and drank rum.
They dreamt exotic dreams, as far away as Galway and Jamaica,
sewing themselves into the fabric of fragrant leather and city.
They sent cats purring from Cov to cities you only saw on telly.

I made Ravi proud when his chamois revealed his reflection in me.
In white paint he saw the sky-blue of his eyes in *a true Cov kid*.
He told his son about Jags as he waxed his knackered Cortina.

I gave Margaret some dignity the day she broke down.
And, just like Marilyn Monroe, the men clamoured around her.
They'd all chipped in for her to leave in a Daimler with elegance.

I was made in Cov on *The Lane.* Forged in tourniquets of smog.
Paperboys chased me on hand me down Choppers –
their Mother's and Father's made us both to perfection.

Antony Owen

Cov Kids
For old friends

I was raised with Jaguars and the Young Wives Club.
Even trees on our Lane had crew cuts so buses could pass.
Back then, we never lived in phones, and left footprints, not hashtags.

I remember us, Cov kids were the finest archers:
Darrol Griffin could gob ten meters and three colours.
All of the girls he tried to impress threw their hair at Jimmy 'The Face'.

I remember us, Cov kids, leaving tattoos of our tyres.
And if we got a scab, we'd hack at it like gum-grey bras in the Odeon.
We all tried the back seat for a snog, but most of us had to wait another summer.

I remember my first kiss was like a soft April rain:
it clung to my lips and left a taste of a season forever gone,
like petrol in a puddle leaves a rainbow – well that was our childhood as Cov Kids.

I was raised with Mark 'The Mouth', making dens for somewhere to hide.
Guess what we found as Cov kids is what we lost in the blue years.
Cov was always grey, but we burned brighter than Phoenixes:
rising up, tearing it down, yet building our characters and …

new Cov Kids with fire in their raging phoenix hearts.

Memoirs of Job Seeker NZ328509B

I awake drowning in the landfill of first light.
Each day gets heavier as I try to carry them quietly, but fail.
Yesterday I stared at an application form and two hours passed.
I'd written a statement of who they want me to be and guess I drifted away.

What makes a grown man curl up like a foetus?
Is it when he's reborn from the cunt of a job centre's door and given a zone to die.
What makes a grown man get smaller each day?
Is it when yawning boys at agencies roll apps and eyes at disappearing people.

I want to report my tragic disappearance.
It happened again this morning when my wife wept in secret to protect me.
Every morning she puts on a brave face and feeds the black dog and elephant.
Her body aches from work and dragging the iron chains of her shadow slave.

The truth of unemployment is the greatest lie you believed:
a chav with eight children from ten different Mothers can be possible;
the migrant who robbed that job and food from an Englishman's mouth.
No, the truth of unemployment is how quickly it eats a person's mind.

The truth of unemployment is the sea of ash the lost awake in.
Some feel the only thing they can control is not life but the other,
like that bloke from Sunderland who Dave659 shared on Twitter,
and that woman outside Poundland at the end of her tether,
telling me her life meant nothing, that she felt, like nothing,
that she was nothing and how she could find nothing.

I had to do something,
and tell you.

Antony Owen

Paradise in Amazon
For Martin Hayes

We live in paradise.
Exotic birds sing from TV Aerials.
This is our cage and we commute to Amazon.

Last week a man dropped dead on barcodes.
He wore a viz-vest and no one noticed.
It took twenty minutes – a long time here.

I am a skilled man.
The agency insisted this is good for me.
If I show willing they might find me proper work.

Three contracts ago
my white skin turned black from oil.
An Iraqi man said it was ironic he was placed there.

We'll die in paradise.
The Iraqi man voted to remain, ironic.
He said in weeks he will weep at the Tigris, lighting fires.

Have you ever heard how we speak to each other in Paradise?
Every Friday we dance in strobe lights and sing aloud,
coloured red, white, pink, like exotic birds.

The Brave Leave Willingly
"Make it a good one"
  – Leanne Bridgewater

Your death is a hinderance:
it twists my heart like a Rubik's cube.
Every side is black and I cannot work it out.

I want to rip out the tongues of my shoes.
Curse the route I never took to you.
Never speak of my failure to help.

I want to punch the white face of a mocking clock.
Tear out the hands and shout: "Fuck you time."
But no, no, I shall raise the cuckoo to wake me gently.

Your death made me stop my car on Leamington Road,
move a fox from roaring road to a lullaby lay-by.
My heart is meat, and you always hated meat.

I want to look at the photograph of you smiling as a baby,
like my baby that I shall raise in the permanent wing;
it is not the earth that kills us but the earthlings.

I want to feel the crematorium of that hug we had in Cov:
by the tree that caught all the bags trapped in a vortex.
I want to say goodbye properly Leanne and never go, just leave.

Antony Owen

A Teacher's Suicide

In the silk rags of cigarette smoke
we wolf whistled the crush teacher.
She never knew who we were, and
neither did we, in nineteen eighty-eight.

I remember snow, grey as P.E whites.
The awkwardness of undressing together,
and loudmouths who puberty quietened in
the race to have a man-cock and the easy shower.

I remember a teacher, who never stopped smiling.
One day, we found out he hung himself for debt.
All the unloved kids loved him, mourned him over.
I learnt from the 'thick ones' the most important lesson.

I remember seeing the dead teacher stare at the sky.
He was feeling sun on his face for a brief moment.
He noticed that I noticed and smiled his lying smile.
That was the night before the night when he became sky.

Before the Rain Came

Our ring road is a forced marriage
of IKEA sky once held together
by medieval beams.

Many times my city has walked through me
and turned to stone in my eyes
when I took a piss on Spon Street.

A pub served mead the old way here.
Landlords made way for baristas
boasting fair-trade on tax free plots.

Our city was made by flames.
The phoenix was a welder's torch.
Men like my Da before the rain came.

Our city was a blank canvas:
two-tones barely mixing,
bleeding separately away from each other.

Many times, my brothers walked past me
down Foleshill Road in the rain,
those colours should have run.

Then Coventry would be grey,
two-tone,
beautiful.

Antony Owen

Closing Libraries in The City of Culture

John lost his job and found a library.
Read fiction to escape real life.
Found himself eventually
when someone read him:
a librarian who saw him.
They made a résumé,
he now bends metal,
reads the lathe and
is safe for a while –
yet industry
is never
fully
safe.

Rashmir lost his country and found
a city of sanctuary, of peace.
A library freed him daily
from displacement from
fires, deaths and rapes.
Rashmir read poems,
by Rumi and Larkin.
Bridges were built.
He saw the light.
Walls crumbled.
Libraries fell &
he was alone,
lost as a lamb.
Sanctuary?
Where?

Cov Kids

Jennifer lost her husband to Alzheimer's.
A library helped them find a moment,
pictures from the blitz returned him.
His tears put out the fires, evacuees
are no different to Asylum seekers.
They search for a safe haven
like libraries, like Earlsdon.
It is time to open minds,
close eyes and think
of nowhere to go.
We are homeless
in Brexit's cage.
Kill a library.
Kill refuge.
Kill peace.
Kill Cov?

Antony Owen

Coventry Street

This city lost another street today.
A baker threw his thumbprints to birds.
Legs of lamb were walked to a skip.

This street was named after a clockmaker.
His hands stroke the bell towers face.
Pigeons swoop for burgers there.

This city progressed today.
A busker buried his symphonies,
walked headless to Starbucks.

My city lost its voice today.
In its stone-grey throat
a song was soulless.

Daily Mail

You portray rats as refugees, like Nazi propaganda.
We take them in, like mothers do, scent to their kin.
They paint our grey city as a portrait of sanctuary.
Take that in for a moment and let it absorb like ink.
You report there is more culture in a yoghurt than in Cov,
like the yoghurt and milk from foodbanks under our ring road?
Or yoghurt adverts on your website interrupting fake journalism?
Did you know that Twitter is a nest where some vultures circle?
In my city is a Rastafarian man washing his hair in a library sink.
He reads books and people then begs for change yet changes us.
It is people like him, with his cap filled with rain and loose change,
that make us the richest city in all the right ways you fail to see.
My grey city was mixed with two-tone to get to this colour,
a colour you can never see. So why not come and feel its pallor.
All of us shall welcome you like real people in the real news.
We are making a tide and a shore, shaping the rocks for all to stay here.

Antony Owen

The Most Beautiful Cov Kids

Are two boys or two girls holding hands and kissing?
They have not yet been told instinctual love is wrong, *but will be*.
All they are doing is showing love without a care in the world.
One of these kids is not a Cov Kid *but they're everywhere:*
in Small Heath, Birmingham, running like colours in banned graffiti.
They shine through the bleach a councillor ordered to rid the stain.
Hell yeah, and Okay Yah, they are the bark of all that is pure:
a Tardis seed of Pippin blossom.

Cov kids are everywhere:
in the sky-blue waters of a pregnant Mum kicking her like Brian Kilcline;
on Latin named streets of Cheylesmore named after people who ended badly.
But look how we start, how we mean to go on, taking the knocks like a winning punch.

Cov kids are everywhere:
in the ancient child evacuee that told her carer from the Wyken of Aleppo what happened.

Coventry Zoo

Our zoo was like a bar fight at the Pink Parrott Nightclub.
Harry the Hippo dragged his keeper into the water.
They had to prise its mouth open.
Years later in the Pink Parrott
a man had his nose bitten off.
They kept the party going.
We Spandau ballerinas
danced bloody-footed
like the zoo keeper.

We loved things in cages and had keepers for them.
Scargill and Maggie had the keys for the cage,
but canaries don't fare well in Coventry.
City Arcade had its birdsong removed:
that was another zoo run by shopkeepers.
We love our keepers in Cov, love em,
but two-tone always freed us, always.
And Maggie was our pigeon –
lifting the blue of her wing
to shit all over us.

Antony Owen

Some Famous Cov Kids

Clive Owen used to be invisible in a dole queue.
it is rumoured that job centre carpets are dreamcatchers,
and if you are lucky enough you might escape joining the pattern.

The Ghosts from Ghost Town are still around Cov doing their gigs.
Joan from Chapelfields is haunted by her husband sometimes.
She doesn't mind though; she loved the black-clothed bones off that man.

Margaret Keenan was our first masked hero to beat Covid,
and this wasn't Gotham but Walsgrave, Coventry.
We don't talk about Pete Waterman.

Poems for People Who Never Read Them

If I was clever enough, I would write a poem about poetry
and watch snowflakes cover footprints of half bent jobseekers
blowing their unemployed breaths into the Coventry moon.

If I was clever enough, I would add important letters after my name
and ask a surgeon from Damascus "Why are you cleaning in ASDA?"
He would tell me he is blessed as I saw his face in my wiped away footprints.

If I was arsed enough, I could sip a wheatgrass latte in Kensington and
launch a collection of poetry on why I love wheatgrass latte so much,
called Why I Love Winter and Wheatgrass Latte (So Much).

If I was loaded, I'd post Princess Charlotte a rattle made of blood diamonds
and invite her Granny to my book launch at the Koh-I-Noor takeaway.
The surgeon from Damascus could photo bomb the money shot.

If I was British enough, I would omit that last stanza and say: "Soz and that,"
or, "Dreadfully sorry Ladies and Gents I seem to have forgotten my place."
I am at my place now watching my cat guarding his territory of fuck all.

If I was poetic enough, I would write poems for people who never read them:
the man across the road with his arse hanging out in a bay of red roses;
my neighbour staring at her dead husband's arms waving to her from pegs.

If I was poetic enough, I would title this poem something really clever like
'The Ballad of Francesca De Montford's Washing Line.'
But, her name aint that posh and she wouldn't give a fuck about this poem.

Antony Owen

Rebellion Song

Walk with me, my love, through the Trump funded Oaks – daubed red to be cut down – and I shall hold your face like a tragic promise in the sold-out wind there. Did you know, trees are betrothed to sky in rings that form an atlas into bark made from oceans that fell on their knees praying from east to west? It's the way she said: "I love you, always have, always will," and these working-class manifestos are forged from all the suns we lived through that lifted and fell like veils of queuing brides dressed in spindle silk for one day in Pakistani meadows. Yes, Pakistan has meadows, it is so much more than just war.

Walk with me, my love, where our friends with wrong tongues shouted hopeless rebellions at a country that cut them down like oaks. Look at the streets where Hombres photographed a moving flag of Britain. Where saltires of market stalls criss-crossed through Small Heath in Braeburn pinks like the colour of his cheeks, yes, the colour of his non-white cheeks. Look at the empty shop wells where that woman, who God forgot, wore a scarf over her face so believers would feed her. Oh man, I believed in God that day when she left fatter. Yes, women who cover their faces there are people like me who really saw you.

Walk with me, my love, through the miasma of pepper sprayed streets and hold your head up high to keep your nose from bleeding. Walk with me to the pinstriped man who popped the world like a blue and green balloon, and ask him to excuse us. Run with me past Trump and Murdoch Boulevard where birds sing, past the curfew. And after our sixty-hour working week, we'll catch the privatised rain in jam-jars and hope no one reports us for stealing the sky.

Sleep by me, my love, and I'll send a contraband text to our friends who now live in enemy states. Dream with me, my love.

www.ingramcontent.com/pod-product-compliance
Lightning Source LLC
Chambersburg PA
CBHW011803040426
42450CB00018B/3455